You can learn more about Author Tania Giguere at Tania's Field of Dreams, Facebook, Amazon Author Pages, Pinterest, Twitter, Tumblr, and Goodreads.

Publishing History

Creepy Crawly Things Paperback

First Addition 2018

ISBN-13: 978-1722044657

CREEPY CRAWLY THINGS

Tania Giguere

We Live In Every Part Of Mother Earth

Honey Bees

Giant Centipedes

Canthigaster Cicada

Tiger Mosquito

Caterpillar

Wasp

Beetle Coleoptera

Orchid Bee

Grasshopper

Walking Leaf

Nimble Caterpillar

Spider and Ladybug

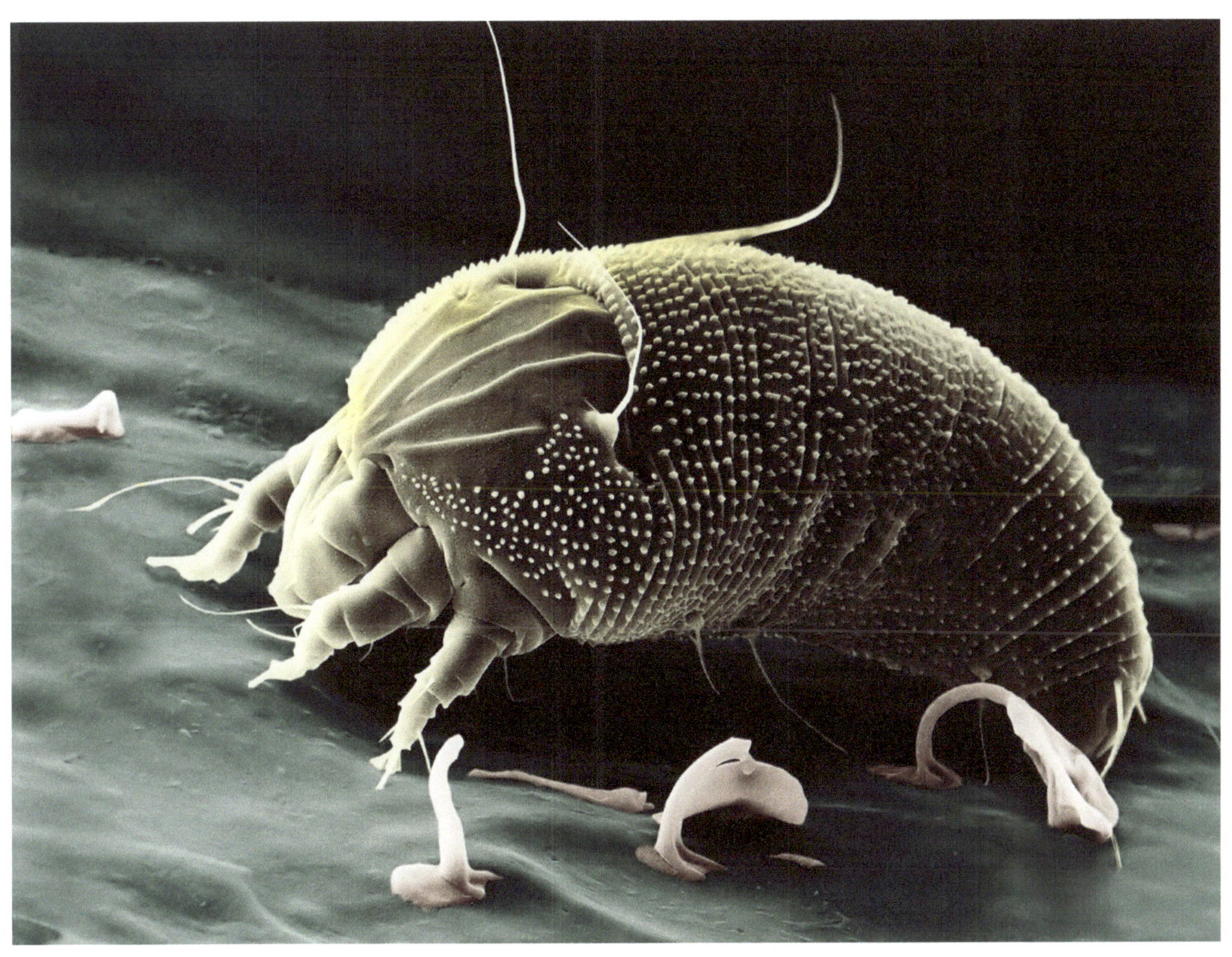

Mite

Jumping Spider

Yellow Spider

Cayenne Tick

Black Scorpion

Kołosz Colored Spider

Scorpio Brown

Beetles

Beetles

Caterpillar

Dragonfly

Fire Ant

Fire Ant

Armadillo Worm Bug

Blue Slug

Earthworm

Glow Worm

Green Tree Snake

Housefly

Ladybug

Beetle Firefighter

Tropical Butterfly

Moth Lepidoptera

Filbert Weevil Bug

Spider Arachnid

Microscopic Bug Bacteria

Assel Porcellio Scaber

Spider Tarantula

Praying Mantis

Walking Stick

Leaf Bug

Baby Spiders

Wasp Nest

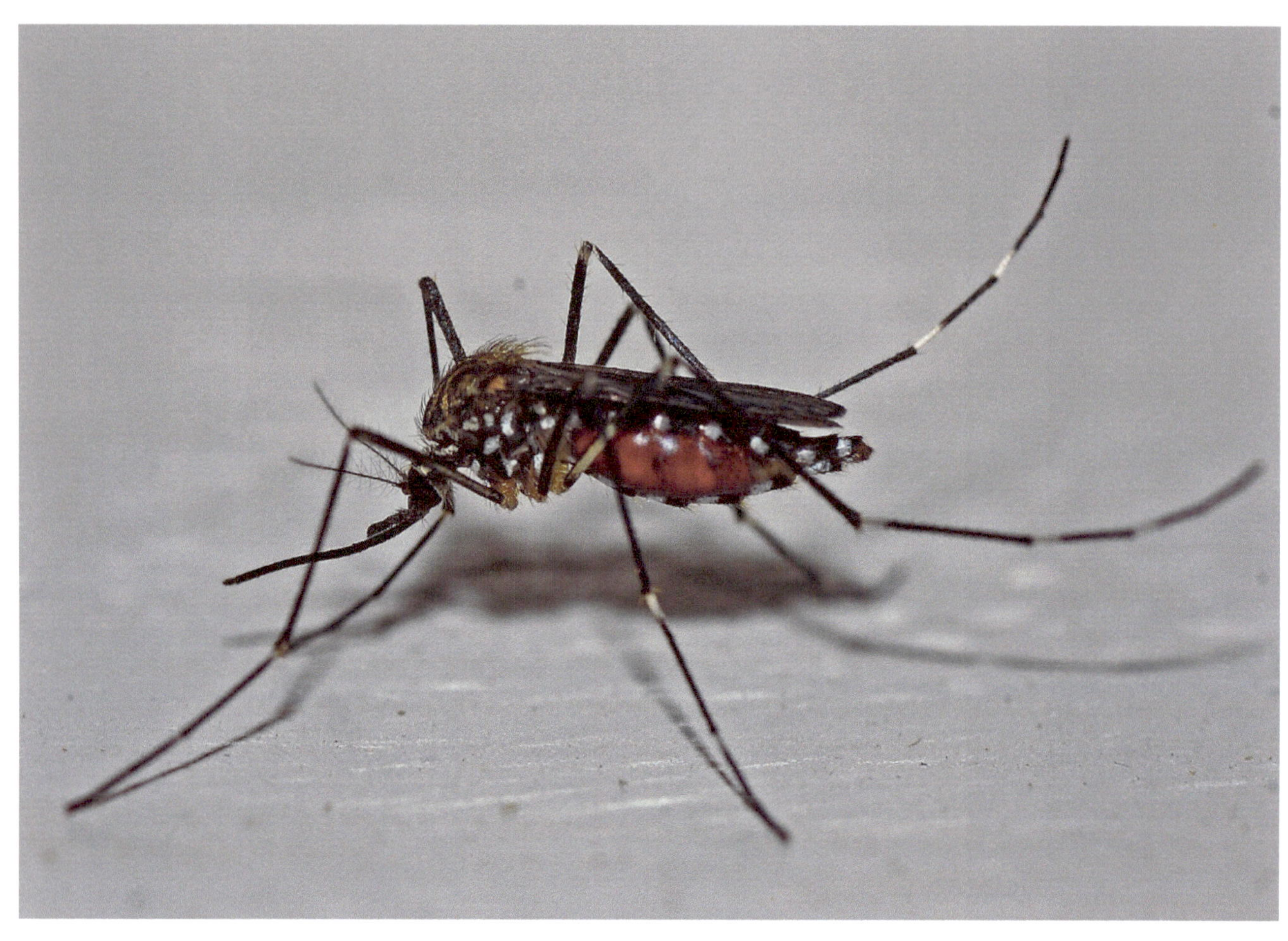

Mosquito with blood

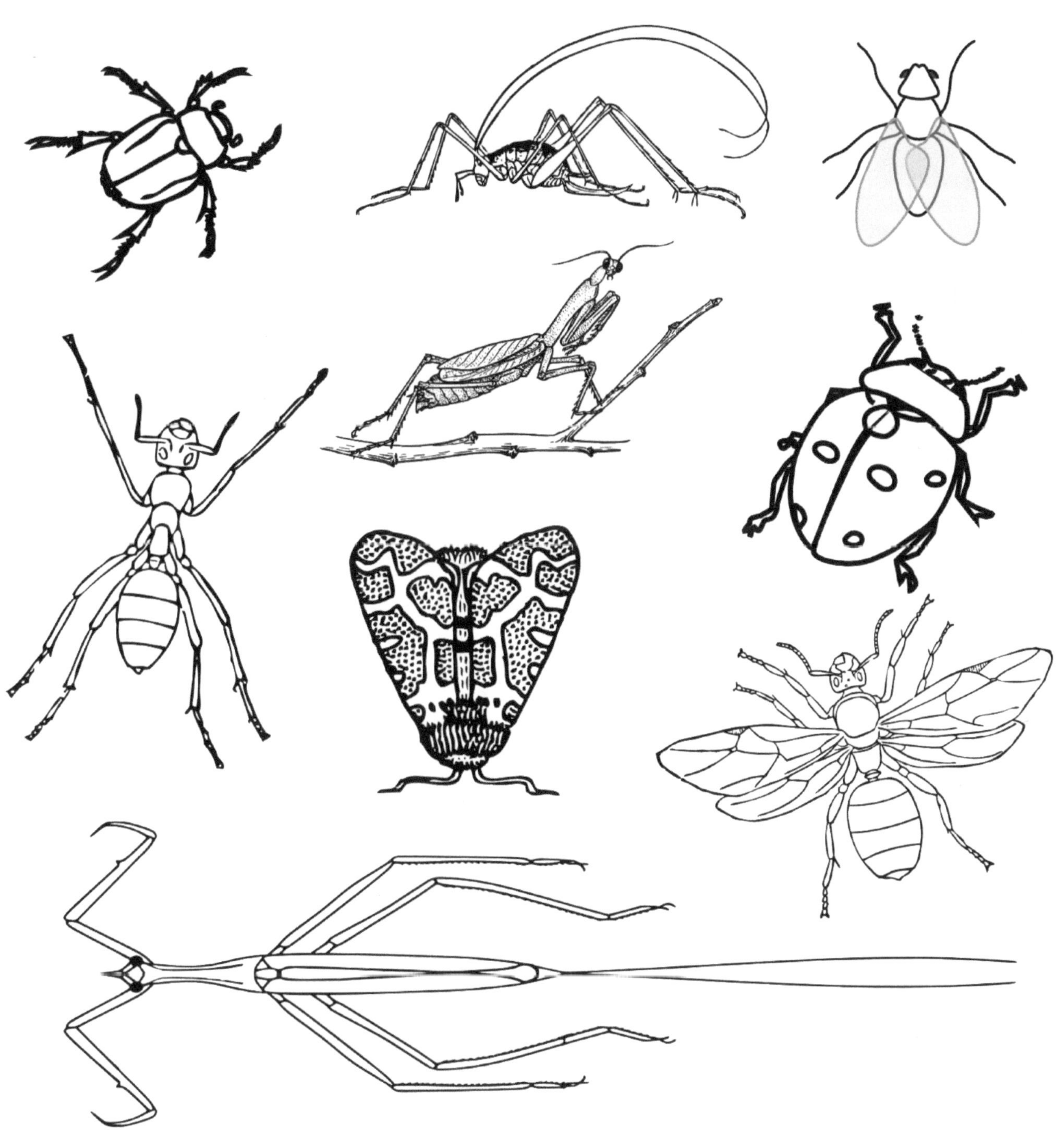

Insects

Pupa Cutworm Moth

Caterpillar Larva

Wax Worm

Firefly Lightning Bug

Water Bug

Hornets

Silkworm Cocoons

Silkworm

Termites

What an amazing place to explore